# Siena
*Travel Guide*

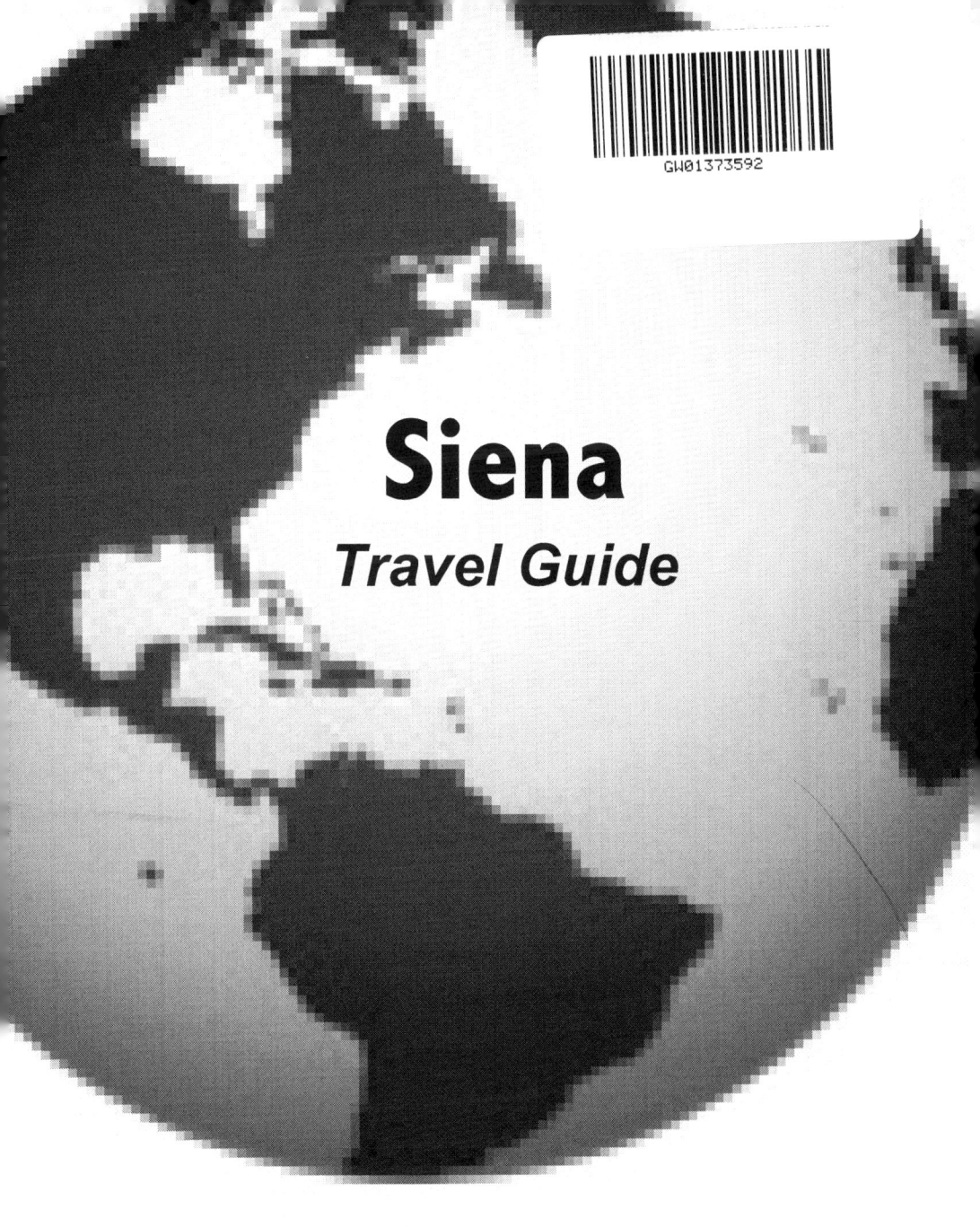

*Quick Trips Series*

No part of this publication may be reproduced, stored in a retrieval system, or transmitted, in any form or by any means without the prior written permission of the publisher, nor be otherwise circulated in any form of binding or cover other than that in which it is published and without similar condition being imposed on the subsequent purchaser. If there are any errors or omissions in copyright acknowledgements the publisher will be pleased to insert the appropriate acknowledgement in any subsequent printing of this publication. Although we have taken all reasonable care in researching this book we make no warranty about the accuracy or completeness of its content and disclaim all liability arising from its use.

Copyright © 2016, Astute Press
All Rights Reserved.

# Table of Contents

## SIENA — 6
- 🌐 CUSTOMS & CULTURE ... 7
- 🌐 GEOGRAPHY ... 13
- 🌐 WEATHER & BEST TIME TO VISIT ... 19

## SIGHTS & ACTIVITIES: WHAT TO SEE & DO — 21
- 🌐 PIAZZA DEL CAMPO ... 22
  - The Palio ... 24
- 🌐 PALAZZO PUBBLICO ... 25
  - Municipal Museum (Museo Civico) ... 26
  - Clock Tower (Torre del Mangia) ... 28
  - Fountain of Joy (Fonte Gaia) ... 30
- 🌐 SIENA CATHEDRAL (DUOMO) ... 31
  - Piccolomini Library ... 33
- 🌐 CHURCH OF SAINT AUGUST (CHIESA DI SANT AGOSTO) ... 34
- 🌐 MEDICI FORTRESS ... 35
- 🌐 PICCOLOMINI PALACE ... 37
- 🌐 PALAZZO DELLE PAPESSE ... 39
- 🌐 SANTA MARIA DELLA SCALA ... 40
- 🌐 NATIONAL PICTURE GALLERY (PINACOTECA NATIONALE) . 43
- 🌐 NATURE TRAIN (TRENO NATURA) ... 46

## BUDGET TIPS — 48
- 🌐 ACCOMMODATION ... 48

Residence Paradiso ...................................................................48
Casa di Antonella .....................................................................49
B&B Quattro Cantoni ..............................................................50
Villa Montarioso ......................................................................51
Fonti di Pescaia .......................................................................52

## 🌐 Restaurants, Cafés & Bars ...............................................53

La Taverna di San Giuseppe ...................................................53
Ristorante Enoteca Millevini ..................................................55
Osteria Enoteca Sotto le Fonti ................................................56
Antica Osteria da Divo ............................................................57
Enoteca I Terzi ........................................................................58

## 🌐 Shopping ............................................................................59

Wednesday Market ..................................................................59
Antichita Mona Agnese ...........................................................60
Bianco e Nero di Staccioli Sonia ............................................61
Falegnameria Artistica ............................................................62
Via di Citta ..............................................................................62

# KNOW BEFORE YOU GO      64

## 🌐 Entry Requirements ........................................................64

## 🌐 Health Insurance .............................................................64

## 🌐 Travelling with Pets .......................................................65

## 🌐 Airports ............................................................................65

## 🌐 Airlines .............................................................................67

## 🌐 Currency ..........................................................................68

## 🌐 Banking & ATMs ............................................................68

## 🌐 Credit Cards ...................................................................68

## 🌐 Tourist Taxes ..................................................................69

## 🌐 Reclaiming VAT .............................................................69

## 🌐 Tipping Policy ................................................................70

## 🌐 Mobile Phones ................................................................70

- 🌐 **Dialling Code** ............................................................................ 71
- 🌐 **Emergency Numbers** ................................................................ 71
- 🌐 **Public Holidays** ........................................................................ 72
- 🌐 **Time Zone** ................................................................................ 72
- 🌐 **Daylight Savings Time** .............................................................. 73
- 🌐 **School Holidays** ....................................................................... 73
- 🌐 **Trading Hours** .......................................................................... 73
- 🌐 **Driving Laws** ............................................................................ 74
- 🌐 **Drinking Laws** .......................................................................... 75
- 🌐 **Smoking Laws** .......................................................................... 75
- 🌐 **Electricity** ................................................................................. 75
- 🌐 **Tourist Information (TI)** ........................................................... 76
- 🌐 **Food & Drink** ............................................................................ 77
- 🌐 **Websites** ................................................................................... 78

# SIENA TRAVEL GUIDE

## Siena

Siena is a medieval Italian city in Tuscany, seventy kilometres south of Florence. It is known for its colourful horse race, Il Palio that is held twice each summer.

Standing on three hills in Northern Italy, Siena's Piazza del Campo is the city's main square and the hub of activity. The city was built to act as a military fortress but

## SIENA TRAVEL GUIDE

today the visitor will fall in love with the city's laid-back lifestyle and its thriving culture.

Take a stroll through the rolling hills to the Benedictine abbey and explore the hillsides as you witness the local customs in this part of rural Italy.

With many of its ancient structures now restored, Siena has been reborn as a tourist attraction in recent years and is regarded by many as one of the best of northern Italy's tourist destinations.

The Il Palio horse race is held in Siena and it's a delightful celebration of the city's heritage. The Il Palio horse race and the city were featured in the James Bond film Quantum of Solace.

# SIENA TRAVEL GUIDE

# 🌍 Customs & Culture

In Roman legend, Siena was founded by Senius Remus and his brother, Romulus (after whom Rome is named). According to the story they were suckled by a wolf from birth. Though this origin story is entangled with mythology, the city embraced it early on, and as such, many representations of the wolf and her babes can be seen throughout its artwork, statues, and buildings. Try to spot some of these less-obvious carvings and artworks as you wander through the winding streets.

Siena maintains a contrada culture, which means that it is organized into wards. Each neighborhood or ward is incredibly tight-knit and has an animal that represents it. The wards were originally formed as battalions for the city's defense, but have maintained a loyalty well beyond any military use.

# **SIENA TRAVEL GUIDE**

Siena is a town which relies primarily on agriculture, and as such, it offers a wide variety of specialties for the hungry visitor. From its fresh seafood offerings straight from the Tuscan coast to its specialty confectioners baking local delicacies to perfection, Siena will not leave anyone hungry. In recent years, the tourism trade has grown tremendously, which offers continuously more enjoyable and comfortable visits for travelers.

In the 12th century, Siena was run by a bourgeois group called the Council of Nine, who vehemently supported the arts. This led to the construction of many of the city's most distinctive buildings in the Sienese-Gothic style, as well as the Sienese school of painting, all of which is still on view and thriving in the city today. Siena was also home to one of Italy's most famous saints, Santa Caterina, and curious

## SIENA TRAVEL GUIDE

travelers can visit many of her former haunts that have been beautifully restored.

The most important event in Siena is certainly the Palio but there are a number of other events and festivals all the year round in this beautiful province. The Carnival of Asciano every February is a traditional carnival involving processions of carnival chariots, folklore activities and music groups. The La Terbbiatura in July is a festival dedicated to agriculture. The weeklong Maggiolata in Val d'Orcia celebrates the coming of May through traditional song and dance. The popular Festival of the Newly Made Olive Oil is celebrated in December whereas the Wine and Oil Week involving free tasting, workshops and conferences on the finest wines and extra virgin olive oil of the region is celebrated in February. Other interesting festivals include the Festival of the Wild Boar every April

## SIENA TRAVEL GUIDE

and the historic harvesting festival of Festa della Trebbiatura every July.

Arts and crafts lovers have a lot to cheer about in Siena. There are many traditional crafts and techniques that have been handed down for many generations and are still practiced in many places throughout the city. Buying one of these artworks means bringing a small piece of Tuscan history back home.

There are a number of workshops, stores, and markets where one can watch these artworks being created or sold. The Duomo of Siena (Tel: +39 0577 45 006) is a traditional ceramic workshop in Via P. A. Mattioli 12 that produces original handcrafted items of the finest quality using some of the ancient techniques. The Vetrate Artistiche Toscane (Tel: +39 0577 48 033) at Via della

# **SIENA TRAVEL GUIDE**

Galluzza 5 is a renowned glass art studio where craftsmen produce exquisitely beautiful stained glass artwork.

Silk painting, papier-mache, batik printing, and mosaic artwork can be bought at Il Girasole (Tel: +39 0577 45 942) at Via S Petro 48. Book lovers can head to Sator Print (Tel: +39 0577 24 74 78) at Piaggia del Giuggiolo to browse through their collection of limited edition handmade books on art. Besides these stand alone stores, there are a number of weekly and annual markets that display and sell different handmade crafts. The Mercantino delle Crete is one such market open on the 2nd Sunday of every month. The Forme nel Verde in San Quirico d"orcia is an international exhibition of sculptures in the magnificent Horti Leonini Garden.

# **SIENA TRAVEL GUIDE**

Music lovers can head to the Siena Jazz Festival - http://www.sienajazz.it/en/ - held every summer, to enjoy some of the finest jazz performances in the city. The world renowned Siena Jazz Foundation (Fondazione Siena Jazz) which is a part of Medici Fortress, puts on concerts in summer in the fort complex. A number of classical concerts are held in Via di Citti throughout the year at the Accademia Musicale Chigiana; it culminates into the week long celebrations in the month of August every year.

The International Guitar Festival every January invites 5 guest musicians every year and pays tribute to the different guitar genres. The Aromatic City festival features jazz, rock, and ethnic music. Opera lovers can enjoy a performance at the grand Monteriggioni Castle. Summer

## SIENA TRAVEL GUIDE

months also sees the hosting of the 'Cinema in Fortezza' where movies are screened outdoors under the stars.

For those looking for a more physically engaging activity, the Tuscan hills can provide the perfect solution. Breathtakingly beautiful, the hills are perfect for a hike on a clear sunny day. A more adrenalin pumping experience would be to visit a football (soccer) match (other than the Palio, of course) at a local stadium. The Siena Football Club - AC Siena - has even played in the first division in the Italian league - one of the finest football leagues in the world. Although the team has relegated to the 2nd division, there is no dearth in the passion and support to the local team and one can enjoy an evening of absolute eccentricity - in a good way if AC Siena wins.

# SIENA TRAVEL GUIDE

## 🌐 Geography

Siena is the capital of the Siena province, situated in Northern Italy. About 70 km south of Florence, Siena is located in the heart of the Tuscan region. This region is known for its rolling countryside, spectacular views, and production of Italian specialties like wines and olive oils.

Most travelers fly into the airports in Pisa or Florence, where buses are available with direct routes to Siena. More budget-friendly travelers opt to fly into Bologna Marconi airport (IATA: BLQ) - http://www.bologna-airport.it and take the Siena bus from there, though it requires an approximately 2.5 hour bus ride. Even lengthier rides can be enjoyable in the daytime or early morning, when the scenery can be viewed at its finest.

# **SIENA TRAVEL GUIDE**

The airport in Pisa International Airport (IATA: PSA) - http://www.pisa-airport.com/ - is the primary airport of the Tuscany region and has regular flights to Paris, Berlin, Munich, Bucharest, Amsterdam, London, and Barcelona. It is located 100 km from Siena. A one-way bus from the Pisa International Airport to Siena costs €15 (there is a discount of €2 on a return ticket). Further details and timetable for the Pisa airport bus service can be found at - http://www.airportbusexpress.it.

Tourist coaches offer multiple services daily. It is best to book in advance with them during the peak tourist season; the timetable and tariff chart for the tourist coaches can be found at - http://www.sienamobilita.it. Another option is to take the train service which is also available from just outside the airport Arrival area. Details of the schedule and fare chart can be found at

## **SIENA TRAVEL GUIDE**

http://www.trainspa.it. Tickets for the Train SPA can be bought at the Tourist Information Desk at the airport. Radio taxis (Tel: 050 54 16 00) are also available from the airport but due to the distance this would be a very expensive option. Private chauffeured cars are available at a price tag of over €100 per trip.

The Florence Airport Peretola (IATA: FLR) - http://www.aeroporto.firenze.it is considered the 2nd most important airport in the Tuscany region and is located about 70 km from Siena. Although there are both bus and train services from the Florence Airport to Siena, it is preferable to take the bus - http://www.ataf.net/, which, not only leave every 30 minutes but also reach Siena in an hour, almost half the time taken by train. The Bus terminal is close to the Central Train Station and is connected directly by the airport shuttle from the airport.

# **SIENA TRAVEL GUIDE**

Try to book a 'Rapida' which does not stop in between at Florence.

Many plan to drive from the airport as Siena is just an hour way. Take the Firenze - Sienna Highway and exit at Sienna Nord to enter the city limits. Private chauffeured cars (€150) are available between 8:00 am and 8:00 pm (20% extra for services between 8:00 pm and 8:00 am). For large groups (5 or more), it would be cheaper to rent a small van / minibus for €220.

Italy is known for its train rides and one can easily get to the Tuscany region (and Siena) from a number of locations all over Italy and Europe through the Trenitalia - http://www.trenitalia.com/ - the Italian railway system. A one way ticket from Rome costs as low as €16 but can go up to €52 during busy weekends and peak tourist season

## SIENA TRAVEL GUIDE

so it is advised to buy tickets in advance to avoid the high prices, or the chance of not getting a reservation.

For those visiting Italy and planning to take the train to Siena, the best option is to get to Florence central station – Santa Maria Novella – one of best connected stations in Italy with direct international connections with Paris, Brussels, Munich, Amsterdam, and Brussels, to name a few. Siena is also connected directly with Chiusi and Grosetto from the south.

Once in Siena, one can see the major attractions at the historic city center by foot; but, Siena is not only about its historic center. The Tuscan hills and neighboring villages and vineyards are major attractions and certainly not to be given a miss by visiting tourists. The city is spread on 3 hills and walking up and down may be quite taxing. It is

## SIENA TRAVEL GUIDE

advisable to wear comfortable shoes if one is planning a long day of walking.

The most convenient way to move around is by car and many plan to drive in to the city. It should be noted that the historic city center is a no-vehicle zone. Hotels issue a slip for their reserved guests to allow a one-time entry for the car through the center to drop the luggage. Either this slip or the reservation slip is mandatory for police to allow the vehicle through the zone. Parking space is not a major problem but the parking rates are quite steep, at times in excess of €30 for a day near the major tourist spots! Details of parking spots in Siena along with the tariff can be found at -

http://www.discovertuscany.com/siena/tourist-info/parking-lots-in-siena.html.

# SIENA TRAVEL GUIDE

Gasoline is also very expensive in Italy with petrol prices reaching as high as €1.25 per liter. One should be very attentive while driving in Tuscany as there are narrow roads and sharp bends and missing one turn may mean driving round a much longer route to get to the destination. Traffic information can be found at CIS Viaggiare Informati (Tel: 1514 - open 24 hrs).

Tra-in offers city bus services for 0.90, which run between the train station and Piazza Gramsci. Details of bus services and the tariff can be found at - http://www.capautolinee.it and http://www.fsbusitalia.it/.

Rental vehicles are available as well. Popular car rental companies in Siena include Auto Europa (Tel: 800 33 440), Europcar (Tel: 800 01 44 10), and Sixt Rent A Car (Tel: 800 900 666). Scooters and mountain bikes are available for rent at Perozzi Noleggi and make a great option for those want to see the city quickly but closely, but being a hilly area, one should be in good physical condition to bike around in Siena. Most of the trains (except Eurostar) have facilities to carry bikes from one destination to another.

# 🌐 Weather & Best Time to Visit

Between the months of May and August are generally the most favorable weather conditions to visit Siena. Temperatures generally range from 15 and 30 degrees Celsius during the summer. July is the warmest month, but travelers should beware that Siena does experience high amounts of humidity. Travelers should plan to drink plenty and dress coolly.

# **SIENA TRAVEL GUIDE**

Temperatures fall the lowest during December, to around an average of 7 degrees Celsius. Autumn is a pleasant, cooler time to visit, but can a rainy season, especially in late Autumn. November is the rainiest month in Siena, although the rains are not typically excessive.

Summertime visitors will find the most activities to do, although the city's beautiful architecture and fascinating museums can be experienced yearlong. Several large festivals and city events take place in the months of July and August, so aim to visit then if you want to take part in these citywide traditions.

**SIENA TRAVEL GUIDE**

# Sights & Activities: What to See & Do

Siena has a discount option for tourists through the Siena Pass - http://www.florence-tickets.com/siena-pass.html?site=absi. The Pass enables a visitor to receive a discount of 50% on the entry charge at many major attractions including the Duomo (Cathedral), Crypt, Piccolomini Library, and Opera Museum, to name a few. The pass holders do not have to stand in line during entry.

# SIENA TRAVEL GUIDE

A Siena Pass valid for 3 days costs €17.20 (reduced price at €5.20 for children).

## 🌍 Piazza del Campo

Piazza del Campo, 1

Tel: +39 0577 29 26 15

Siena's main square is an open recreation area. It is restricted from motorists, so you won't have to worry about navigating dicey traffic stops. The square is home to several landmarks, from the Fountain of Joy to the Tower of Eater. It is a great central spot for meeting and socializing. Several cafes line the square where you can sit outside, enjoy the ambience of the town, and people-watch. Street performers are often spotted in the square, especially during busier summer months. Being a part of

## SIENA TRAVEL GUIDE

the historic province of Siena, it is listed in the UNESCO World Heritage List.

Established in the 13th century, the Piazza del Campo is considered as one of the foremost medieval squares, primarily for its architectural beauty. The formation of this square not only coincided with the growth of this medieval city, but also with its assertion of communal power. The area was an important seat of commerce and financial activities were concentrated along the present day Via dei Banchi Sotto and Via dei Banchi Sopra.

The Piazza del Campo is shaped like a shell and is surrounded by the Torre del Mangia and Palazzo Pubblico, along with the Fonte Gaia - the Fountain of Joy - at its northwest edge. The square itself was a marketplace and was divided into 9 sections symbolizing

## SIENA TRAVEL GUIDE

the rule of The Nine (Noveschi) that governed the province in the 13th and 14th centuries. One can also see a late Gothic Chapel at the foot of the wall of the Palazzo Pubblico built after the city recuperated from the jaws of the Black Death in the mid 14th century.

The architectural design of the square also symbolized the unity of the different noble families. The red bricked paving arranged in a fishbone style is lined with the palazzo signorili that have unified rooflines unlike the earlier town houses that reflected communal strife. The palazzo signorili used to house the families of the Saracini, the Sansedoni, and the Piccolomini. The uniformity of these late Gothic houses also brought in a balance of the square that enhanced its aesthetic beauty manifold.

# SIENA TRAVEL GUIDE

# The Palio

The Palio is a famous horse race that all districts or "contrade" compete in on July 6th and August 16th of every year. The tradition dates back to August 16, 1656, when it was first held to celebrate the apparition of the Virgin Mary near the old houses belonging to Provenzano Salvani, so it was named "Madonna di Provenzano." It later was run for "Madonna dell'Assunta" who is said to be the patroness of Siena because she was thought to have protected the city against the Florentines in 1260 at the battle of Monteaparti.

The contrada each have their government, coat of arms, emblems, representatives, and traditions, all of which is on full display at the Palio race. Be sure to look for the corner of San Martino, an especially dangerous spot for

### SIENA TRAVEL GUIDE

riders that the locals pad with mattresses to make the race safer. The square is transformed into a racetrack by being filled in with a layer of earth for riders to race on. Before the race itself, there is a colorful and musical parade with riders and bands representing their districts. Seating is arranged wherever it can be found - first, as stadium seating rising from the square, but you will also find spectators lounging in windows, balconies, and rooftops. You may be wondering what glory comes with winning this race, but it is only for a simple hand painted banner that these neighborhoods compete.

## 🌑 Palazzo Pubblico

One of the most dominating buildings lining the Piazza del Campo is the Palazzo Pubblico - the town hall. Built in the late 13th century, this red brick and stone structure is built in the Italian medieval style with strong Gothic influences.

# SIENA TRAVEL GUIDE

The 102 m high Torre de Mangia - bell tower - was added in the mid 14th century.

The town hall used to be the seat of the Council of Nine that governed the province of Siena. Like many other Italian buildings, the town hall has beautiful frescoes that cover its walls and ceilings. These frescoes and other works of art in the building are displayed in the town hall in the Museo Civico or the Municipal Museum section.

## Municipal Museum (Museo Civico)

Piazza del Campo 1

53100 Siena

Tel: +39 0577 29 22 23

Regarded as the city's art museum, the Museo Civico

## SIENA TRAVEL GUIDE

houses all manner of works from the renowned Sienese school of art. There is art to be seen in the building itself, the Sala Monumentali Grand Chambers are astounding, as is the former meeting place for the General Council of the Republic of Siena. In the Sala dei Nove, you will find the largest frescoes of the Middle Ages.

Unlike the religious frescoes that are popular in many Italian churches and religious monuments, the town hall has secular frescoes as it was commissioned by the administrators of the city and not by any religious authority.

The most famous of these frescoes is the 3-panel The Allegory and Effects of Good and Bad Government by the renowned 14th century painter Ambrogio Lorenzetti. One of the 3 panels - the Allegory of Bad Government and Its

## **SIENA TRAVEL GUIDE**

Effects on Town and Country - has special historical significance as it showed the first evidence of the existence of the sand hourglass - an instrument used for timekeeping but without any record of its date and place of invention.

Although many of the frescoes are badly damaged, one can still have a feel of the beauty of this style of artwork while walking through the Sala Della Pace (Hall of Nine) and the Sala del Mappamondo (Great Council Hall).

More rooms have reopened recently to show the Quadreria, many works from famous Sienese artists including detached frescoes and paintings on wood and canvas. The upper floor of the museum overlooks the Southern face of Siena and offers a beautiful view.

# SIENA TRAVEL GUIDE

There is an entry fee of €8.

## Clock Tower (Torre del Mangia)

While in the Palazzo Pubblico, a must-do activity is climbing the tower overlooking the main part of city, including Piazza del Campo and the southern half of Siena. From this tower, you can view over the city's walls and see the countryside beyond it. Because of the size of the tower, only small crowds are allowed at a time. Waiting time can be lengthy, but is well worth it for the spectacular view.

The tower is 88 m tall. During its completion, it was purposely made taller than its Florence counterpart thus making it the tallest tower in Italy of the time. The tower got its nickname - Tower of the Eater - from its first guardian who used to spend all his money on food! The

## **SIENA TRAVEL GUIDE**

marble loggia - Capella di Piazza - was added after the bubonic plague killed nearly half the population of Siena. Originally made of wood, the loggia was converted into a marble vault in 1468.

The mechanical clock was added to the tower in 1360. The tower has 3 bells with the largest one being called the Sunto.

The design and execution of the Torre del Mangia has inspired many towers and monuments in Europe and the USA, the most prominent being the Dock Tower in the UK, the Old Joe Tower in the University of Birmingham (UK), the Pilgrim Monument in Massachusetts (USA), and the clock tower in the ICADE School in Madrid (Spain).

# SIENA TRAVEL GUIDE

Entry fee to the tower is €6; free entry for child below 6 years. The tower is open from 10:00 am - 7:00 pm; it closes at 4:00pm between November and March. It is closed on Dec 25.

## Fountain of Joy (Fonte Gaia)

The Fonte Gaia, or Fountain of Joy, gets its name from the feeling and celebration that took place when residents of Siena first saw the water burst forth from the fountain in 1419. This magnificent landmark fountain was designed in 1419 in the same spot as an old fountain from 1346. The water for this fountain comes from a spring in the surrounding countryside and must go through 25 kilometers of passages built in the Middle Ages known as the Bottini. Charles V is believed to have exclaimed after the seeing the fountain and learning of its mechanism that

# **SIENA TRAVEL GUIDE**

Siena was actually 2 beautiful cities, one above the ground and the other underground.

Built in Gothic and Renaissance style, the fountain is made of white marble and has beautiful sculptures adorning it. Some believe that the fountain was dedicated to the Virgin Mary – the patron of Siena and the bride of God. The decorative panels adorning the fountain have gone through many restorations and replacements over the centuries. The present frame of the fountain along with a number of other statues was constructed by Jacopo della Quercia in 1419. 1858 saw a major restoration where the marble panels and statues of Jacopo were replaced by a number of statues by Tito Sarrocchi depicting the stories and mythologies of ancient Rome. The original statues by Jacopo are kept at the old Ospedale di St Maria della Scala near the Piazza Duomo.

# SIENA TRAVEL GUIDE

# 🌎 Siena Cathedral (Duomo)

This façade of this famous cathedral is said to be one of the most impressive in all of Italy. It is a piece of stunning architecture that you won't want to miss. The cathedral's origins date back to 1196, when the cathedral mason's guild first began planning and construction of the structure. A later and much larger addition was halted in 1348 due to the Black Death, but the outer walls that are its remains can still be seen to the south of the cathedral. The west façade is its most impressive, with three huge entrances and a large brass sun featured in the middle, a stunning example of Sienese style and craftsmanship. The Duomo is built in a French Gothic, Romanesque, and Classical style.

The striking beauty of the inside of this cathedral comes largely from its black and white striped marble columns.

# **SIENA TRAVEL GUIDE**

These colors were chosen because they are the colors of the Sienese coat of arms. Don't miss the area under the choir, which houses frescoes of the Old Testament and life of Christ. These were discovered during a renovation and are thought to be the entryway from an earlier church on the same site. Original marble inlaid floors are exquisite, but only viewable for about three months of the year, ending in October.

The cathedral offers rooftop access on a timed basis. It can often be crowded, but is worth the wait. Virtual tours on tablets are also being offered. An all-in-one ticket will get you access to all parts of the cathedral, including the crypt downstairs.

The Duomo is open from 10:30 am in the morning. Its closing hours change depending on the season; it is open until 7:30 - 8:00 pm in the summer months and closes by 6:30 pm between Nov & Feb. It opens at 1:30 pm on Sundays and holidays. There are special opening hours during the pavement exhibition (Aug to Oct) when it is open until midnight.

## Piccolomini Library

The library of Siena Cathedral is housed of the back of the New Cathedral. You'll first notice the colorful, gorgeous frescoes that tell the story of Siena's cardinal Enea Silvio Piccolomini, who later became Pope Pius II. Piccolomini's nephew commissioned the library in 1492 to house his uncle's manuscripts and books. The library now features many music manuscripts, lit up on display.

**SIENA TRAVEL GUIDE**

# 🌐 Church of Saint August (Chiesa di Sant Agosto)

Prato di San Agostino Town Centre

Tel: +39 0577 38 57 86

First built in 13th century, this gorgeous Gothic church located next to the Via di Citta will give you history and beauty. The church itself has undergone many renovations, but its most striking changes happened during the 18th century after a fire destroyed most of the interior. In 1755, Luigi Vanvitelli, architect to the King of Naples, restored the church to the glory it is seen in today.

The building is open to the public during several times of the day in tourist season, and is well worth the visit. Down the street from the Collegio Tolomei, the church houses many stunning art works. The most impressive of these are the frescoes of the Nativity of Mary and the Nativity of Christ, both attributed to Francesco di Giorgio.

Above the altar, you'll find The Epiphany, a large canvas painting by one of the Italian Renaissance's most famous painters, Sodoma. Il Sodoma, or Giovanni Antonio Bazzi, was known for taking the High Renaissance style and combining it with more traditional Sienese art. The church also houses his work, The Adoration of the Magi.

There is an entry of €2.50.

## 🌍 Medici Fortress

The Fortezza Medicea or Medici Fortress is a mid 16th century fort that was commissioned by Duke Cosimo before he became the first Grand Duke of Tuscany. The fort is also known as the Fort of St Barbara. Located to the north of central Siena, the fort complex was initially 'L' shaped but was later transformed into its current rectangular shape.

The construction of the fort commemorated the defeat of the city of Siena to its archrival Florence in the Battle of Marciano in 1554. The fort was built at the site of a citadel after the Florentine Duke Cosimo wanted to strengthen his grip over the ever-revolting Sienese people. It was also a gesture to deny them independence from the Florentine administration.

The fort was demilitarized in the late 18th century and it was restored in 1937 to allow access to the city's public. The entrance of the fort is on the north eastside - facing Florence. The fort has an outer perimeter of 1.5 km with imposing brick ramparts on all 4 corners. The inside walls are topped with huge pathways and are lined with trees and benches.

The fort stands in between the stadium and the Lizza Gardens. A newly erected statue of St Catherine – the city saint, adorns the southeast side facing the city of Siena. Today, it has been restored into a park which not only house an enoteca (a commercial outlet for the wine industry) and the popular Siena Jazz Foundation; it is also a popular venue to numerous exhibitions and concerts throughout the year.

# 🌐 Piccolomini Palace

Built in 1459 in Pienza, the Piccolomini Palace was the summer residence of Pope Pius II, Enea Silvio Piccolomini. The building, designed by the famous

## SIENA TRAVEL GUIDE

architect Brenardo Rossellino, is the first example of Renaissance architecture. The complex was designed to reflect Pius II's ambitious project for an ideal city. The Piccolomini family lived in the complex until as late as 1962 when it was transferred to the Ente morale di Siena Società di Esecutori di Pie Disposizioni.

The palace is built with the theme of relationship between nature and landscape. The portico at the back of the palace has stunning views of the Monte Amiata and Valdorcia; on the ground floor is a square walled hanging-garden, the first of its kind in Renaissance architecture. This harmonious balance of nature and architecture was so striking that it got the locality its name Pienza – City of Pius.

# **SIENA TRAVEL GUIDE**

The ground level of the palace has an inner courtyard with many exhibition stations. The first floor has the appartemento nobile where the halls open on to the various rooms including the dining room, the study, the music room, the weapons room, the library, and multiple bedrooms. The piano nobile rooms, also on the same floor, have beautifully preserved and restored antiques, paintings, and objects d'art from that period. Located exactly below the piano nobile rooms is a large bookshop with a wide selection of materials and publications on Pius II, the palace, and the territory of Pienza. The Palace is also a popular venue for exhibitions and classical music concerts.

The Palazzo is open from 10:00 am - 4:30 pm; it closes after 6:00 pm between March 15 & October 15. The

Palazzo is closed from Jan 7 to Feb 14 and from Nov 16 to Nov 30.

## Palazzo delle Papesse

Via di Citta 126

53100 Siena

Tel: +39 0577 28 10 41

Caterina Piccolomini, sister of Pope Pius II, had this palazzo built between 1460 and 1495 with a design by Bernardo Rossellino. The palazzo is three floors and is built in the Florentine Renaissance style. Neo-Renaissance frescoes were added later when the palazzo was acquired by the Bank of Italy in 1884. Be sure to catch the second floor terrace view of the façade of the Duomo. Financed by the Siena town council and private sponsors, the palazzo was reopened as a contemporary art gallery in the late 1990s. There are three main spaces: the exhibition area, the Bookshop (designed by Luca Pancrazi), and the temporary exhibition area. The gallery offers many changing exhibitions and offers classes to promote an interest in contemporary art. It is located just off the Via di Citta.

## 🌐 Santa Maria della Scala

Piazza delle Duomo

53100 Siena

Tel: +39 0577 29 22 15

http://www.santamariadellascala.com

Founded in the 9th century, the Santa Maria della Scala - often referred to as simply the Ospedale - was one of the oldest running hospitals in Europe until its services were suspended some years ago. The museum of today once

## SIENA TRAVEL GUIDE

catered to the poor people, sick pilgrims, and abandoned children. Run by the donations of the wealthy noblemen and businessmen, the hospital was administered by a rector with his team of Christian 'brothers'. Today it has reinvented itself as one of the primary art hubs of Siena.

The Ospedale, located near the Duomo, is believed to have been found by a cobbler in 898. A papal decree in 1193 made the hospital independent of the Cathedral. During the mid 14th century the hospital acquired several sacral relics including part of Virgin Mary's veil and a nail from the Cross of Christ. It is believed that these acquisitions were done to increase the pilgrim travel in this area.

By the end of the 13th century, the hospital not only expanded its operations, it also split up its functions like

## SIENA TRAVEL GUIDE

medical services, shelters for the pilgrims, and many others. Another major turning point came in the 18th century when the hospital became a part of the university. It was opened to the public as a museum in 1995. Restoration work is ongoing and with each completed phase, more sections are being made accessible to the public.

With over 20000 sq m spread over 4 levels (presently 12000 sq m is open to the public), the Santa Maria della Scala is a treasure chest of Italian art, mainly in the form of frescoes that adorn its walls and ceilings. The exterior frescoes have unfortunately not been preserved but the interior frescoes reflect the style and art of the period. Although many painters have contributed to the artwork, the primary ones are Simone Martini, and the borthers Pietro Lorenzetti and Ambrogio Lorenzetti. The frescoes

## SIENA TRAVEL GUIDE

mainly depict the life of Virgin Mary – from her birth to her betrothal and beyond.

Another attraction are the altar pieces. Many of these altar pieces were created after the devastating Black Death. Four of the major pieces that can still be seen are the Assumption of the Virgin, The Reliquary Shutters of Andrea Gallerani, the Birth of the Virgin, and the Purification of the Virgin.

Level 4 of the Piazza Duomo has access to the Santissima Annunziata Church, the old Sacristy, the Chapel of the Mantle, and the Chapel of Our Lady. It is at this level that one can see the famous 15th century frescoes. The rooms on the sides of the hall were used as hospital rooms that have been renovated for museum displays. The lower level (Level 3) has access to the

# SIENA TRAVEL GUIDE

courtyard which leads to the famous Fonte Gaia – Fountain of Joy - and the Fienile – a medieval hay-loft. The Corticella – little courtyard – in Level 1 has access to the tunnels to the underground archeological museum.

A visit to the hospital / museum is a must not only to enjoy the art but also to experience thousands of years of Tuscan history under one roof. The narrow corridors, labyrinthine tunnels cut out of tufa stone (soft volcanic rock), monumental rooms, and vaulted ceilings create a feeling of awe to every visitor. Coupled with the mark left by some of the master painters of the period, the Santa Maria della Scala is surely one of the highlights of Siena.

The Museum is open from 10:00 am to 4:30 pm between Oct 16 and Mar 16 and closes at 6:30 pm between Mar 17 and Oct 15.

# 🌐 National Picture Gallery (Pinacoteca Nationale)

Palazzo Buonsignori

Siena

Tel: +39 0577 41 246

http://www.spsae-si.beniculturali.it

Housed in the 14th century Palazzo Buonsignori since 1932, the Pinacoteca Nationale or National Picture gallery has one of the finest collections of paintings in Siena. It is a national museum and displays Italian paintings from the Renaissance and late medieval period.

The Palace was originally the residence of the Pannocchieschi family. Although built in the 15th century, the palace has a neo-medieval façade built in the 19th century influenced by the Palazzo Pubblico. Like many

## SIENA TRAVEL GUIDE

other buildings in Siena, the ground floor of the palace is made of stone where as the upper two floors are brick laden. Surmounted by crenellations, the elegantly designed trifore windows on the upper 2 floors open up into the façade.

The gallery today has one of the most extensive collections of Sienese paintings. The collection was started in the late 18th century by Joseph Ciaccheri. Over the next few decades it was enlarged through many donations and bequests. The collections became a property of the state in 1932, 2 years before the gallery was officially opened at the present venue. The collections grew in 1977 and since then the gallery has in its collection the likes of Spannocchi and Durer. Along with the acquisitions of several Flemish and Nordic paintings, 1977 also saw the opening of the Hall of

## **SIENA TRAVEL GUIDE**

Sculptures with its collections by the Sienese masters of the 14th and 15th centuries.

Important works of art in the gallery include the Polyptych N. 28 by Duccio di Buoninsegna, the Annunciation by Ambrogio Lorenzetti, the Christ at the Column by Il Sodoma, and the Mystic Marriage of St Catherine by Michelion de Besozzo. There are 73 images of artwork in the Web Gallery of Art.

The gallery is open to the public from Tues to Sat from 8:15 am to 7:15 pm; and Sundays, Mondays, and holidays from 9:00 am to 1:00 pm. There is an entry fee of €4.

**SIENA TRAVEL GUIDE**

# 🌐 Nature Train (Treno Natura)

Information Center: Via Camollia 130

53100 Siena

Tel: +39 0577 48 003

http://www.trenonatura.terresiena.it/treno-vapore.html

The Nature Train is a full day train ride on a steam engine train through the beautiful outskirts and villages of the Sienese province. Each train ride coincides with a festival, special event, or fair, and the train journeys to a village or town where the passengers and guests can celebrate with the locals. Buses or other modes of transport are provided to take the guests from the station to the destinations. Originally, the Nature Train ran only from May to October, but with growing demand, one can now enjoy a ride in any season – of course, depending on if a trip is scheduled.

## **SIENA TRAVEL GUIDE**

Popular events when the train schedules a ride include the Maggiolata, the Crete Cheese Festival, and the Amiata Christmas market. Ticket prices and reservation details vary from one trip to another. Details of the schedule, ticket price, and reservation are posted on the website. While booking the train ticket one should clarify if the bus ticket (from the train station to the destination of the event) is included or not.

# SIENA TRAVEL GUIDE

## Budget Tips

## 🌐 Accommodation

## Residence Paradiso

Via del Paradiso, 16 Siena

Tel: +39 0577 11 12 20

http://www.residenceparadiso.siena.it

## SIENA TRAVEL GUIDE

Located close to the San Domenico Church in the historic- center of Siena.

This beautifully decorated guesthouse has 12 rooms with a kitchenette and washing machine. Private parking is available. It is also close to public transport, the bus station being only 100 m away. There is a terrace with beautiful views, perfect for a summer morning tea.

There are both ensuite and non-ensuite rooms. Daily rate for a single room starts from €35, and for a double room from €45. The rooms can also be booked on a weekly basis at a discount.

## Casa di Antonella

Via delle Terme, 72

Siena

## **SIENA TRAVEL GUIDE**

Offering 5 bedrooms with beautiful frescoes and a view of the Cathedral dome, the Casa delle Antonella is a guesthouse that gives the perfect feel of an Italian holiday. The location is ideal for those who are planning to visit the neighboring villages of Siena. Free car parking is available. There is free Wi-Fi and Internet access.

Room rates start from €60. Breakfast is included and is served in the living room between 8:00 am and 9:30 am. Check in is from 11:00 am to 8:00 pm.

## **B&B Quattro Cantoni**

Via San Pietro, 30

Siena

Tel: +39 0577 432 27

http://www.quattrocantonisiena.it

# **SIENA TRAVEL GUIDE**

The B& Quattro Cantoni is located next to the National Gallery and is a short walk away from the Piazza del Campo, so one is right amidst the attractions of Siena. It is housed in a beautiful 14th century renovated building.

With only 3 rooms, it is best to pre-book the rooms before coming here. The 3 rooms, named Sara, Marta, and Anna, are double rooms with a vaulted ceiling and typical Italian décor. If visiting during the celebrations of Palio, one can watch the historic walk from the Marta and Sara rooms. Both these rooms have double glazing for soundproofing. All 3 rooms are ensuite and come with complimentary toiletries. Pets are allowed.

Room rates start from €60 for single occupancy and €75 for double occupancy in the low season. It goes up to €70 and €95 respectively in the high tourist season. Palio night packages (4 nights) can be bought for €440 for single occupancy and €660 for double occupancy. Breakfast is included in the room rates.

## Villa Montarioso

Via Montarioso, 35

Siena

Tel: +39 0577 58 85 26

http://www.villamontarioso.com/

Located 4 km away from the historic town center of Siena, the Villa Montarioso is housed in a 19th century villa inside a beautiful park in Palio. It has 21 elegantly decorated rooms, some providing stunning views of the romantic Tuscany hills. Facilities include elevator, free parking, free Wi-Fi, and non-smoking rooms. The hotel can be easily reached in the airport shuttle.

There are single, double, triple, and quadruple rooms equipped with a minibar, safe, and LCD TV, and hairdryer. Room rates start from €65. Breakfast is included.

## Fonti di Pescaia

Strada di Pescaia

4 via Chiarugi,

1 Siena

Tel: +39 3485 70 30 44

http://www.fontidipescaia.com

The Fonti di Pescaia is a guesthouse located about half a km from the edge of the historic town center of Siena.

## SIENA TRAVEL GUIDE

There are a variety of single, double, and triple rooms, both ensuite and non-ensuite.

The rooms and packages are suitable for the individual traveler as well as groups of up to 15 people. All rooms and bathrooms are designed in typical Tuscan style. Rooms are equipped with free Wi-Fi. There is a private garden and free parking.

Price per night for a double room with attached bathroom starts from €55 that goes up to €75 in the peak season. Cancellations must be done 72 hours prior to the booked date to avoid being charged. The guesthouse only accepts cash (on arrival). Check in is only between 3:00 pm and 6:00 pm.

**SIENA TRAVEL GUIDE**

## 🌐 Restaurants, Cafés & Bars

## La Taverna di San Giuseppe

Via Giovanni Dupre 132

53100 Siena

Tel: +39 0577 422 86

http://www.tavernasangiuseppe.it/

Located just 400 m from the historic Piazza del Campo, the La Taverna is a restaurant with a Tuscan décor and cuisine. It is located in a part of town dating back to the 12th century and the wooden furnishings and candle lit tables play an integral part in making the patrons feel an old world charm. The wine cellar is hand sculpted inside an Etruscan house of the Middle Ages and stores wines of 500 different Italian brands – both local and national.

# SIENA TRAVEL GUIDE

The cuisine is typical Italian and includes home-made pasta, ravioli, and pici, often prepared according to the original ancient recipes. The prosciutto, tagliata (T-bone steak), and tiramisu are specially recommended. A typical meal costs between €25 - 40. It is open Mon to Sat from 12:00 noon to 2:30 pm and from 7:00 pm to 10:00 pm. It is closed on Sundays. The dinner times are strictly maintained so it is best to do a reservation and be on time.

## Ristorante Enoteca Millevini

Fortezza Medicea 1

5300 Siena

Tel: +39 0577 247 121

http://www.ristorantemillevini.it/

The Ristorante Enoteca Millevini is located in the vaults of

## SIENA TRAVEL GUIDE

the Medicea Fortress and offers Italian cuisine. The venue is well known for wine tasting and the restaurant certainly lives up to it with a wide range of wines on its menu. One can also get the wine shipped to foreign locales. Excellent service, delicious food, and a wonderful atmosphere have made it a favorite with many patrons over the years. The restaurant has a multilingual staff and can handle large groups.

Vegetarian starters like eggplant in tomato soup starts from €6. Starters start from €10 and include delicacies like citrus scented ricotta. Main courses are priced between €10 -14. The tuna tartare is recommended. A typical meal in this restaurant would cost around €30 without alcohol/wine.

# Osteria Enoteca Sotto le Fonti

Via Esterna di Fontebranda 114

53110 Siena

Tel: +39 0577 22 64 46

http://www.sottolefonti.it/


This restaurant serving Italian cuisine is located only 10 minutes (walking) from the Piazza del Campo. One can also take the escalators from the Siena Cathedral. Perfect for a snack or a relaxing dinner, the restaurant caters well to all ranges of clients, from romantic couples to families with children. There is a toy area, changing tables, and a kid's menu for groups with children. It has a very cozy décor and some stunning views of the Tuscan landscape.

## SIENA TRAVEL GUIDE

Run as a family-owned business, the chef (Roberto) prepares the food in a traditional homely Tuscan style. The food includes popular Tuscan specialties like the pici, Senese vegetable soup, and ribollita. This is the perfect place to try the local delicacies including Cinta Senese, Pecorino cheese, and fresh truffles. The restaurant also has over 100 varieties of wine. A typical meal in this restaurant costs between €20 - 40. It is open from 12:30 pm – 2:30 pm and from 7:30 pm – 10:30 pm.

## Antica Osteria da Divo

Via Franciosa 25 – 29

53100 Siena

Tel: +39 0577 28 43 81

http://www.osteriadadivo.it/eng/chi-siamo.htm

This 20-seater Italian restaurant is located close to the

## SIENA TRAVEL GUIDE

historic center and is popular not only for its food but also for its décor. The dining space is inside ancient Etruscan rooms that were cut out from soft volcanic rocks (tufa stone), bringing forth a culinary experience of a lifetime for its guests. The close distance from the major attractions of Siena also make it a perfect place to grab a quick bite.

The restaurant has a variety of Tuscan delights especially non-vegetarian dishes including roasted quail covered with Parmesan fondue (€8), steamed lobster with vegetables (€14), and the rolled pork in flavored spinach and potato puree (€22). The very popular dessert menu includes Senese pecorino cheese with honey and fig jam (€10) and dark chocolate cake in pistachio ice-cream (€7). It also serves a wide variety of wine.

**SIENA TRAVEL GUIDE**

# Enoteca I Terzi

Via dei Termini 7

Siena

Tel: +39 0577 443 29

http://www.enotecaiterzi.it/

This popular wine bar (enoteca) gets its name from its location – it is located exactly at the junction of the 3 terzi of Siena – Terzo di Camollia, Terzo di San Martino, and Terzo di Citta. This modern wine bar housed inside brick vaults of a 20th century stone tower is very popular with the working crowd – especially for a quick lunch or a relaxed business meeting.

The menu is changed every 15 days and one can enjoy a variety of dishes here made from fresh raw materials. The rich selection of wines number nearly 1800 and one can buy as well as taste wine from this place. A typical meal costs about €18. It is open from Mon to Sat from 11:00 am – 1:00 am. It is closed on Sundays.

## 🌐 Shopping

### Wednesday Market

One of the largest outdoor markets in Italy, this place is a shopper's haven. Local artisans sell food, wine, clothing, and much more at this market.

It is located near the Piazza del Campo towards Stadio Comunale around Fortezza Medicea. The market is open from 7:00 am to 2:00 pm although most of the shops open after 8:00 am. As the market is in a hilly area, it is best to wear comfortable shoes. For cheese lovers, this is the perfect place to pick up a variety of some of Italy's world famous cheeses.

## Antichita Mona Agnese

60 Via di Chitta

Siena

Located in the famous Via di Chitta shopping street in Siena, the Antichita Mona Agnese is regarded as one of the best places to buy antiques in town. Along with a variety of artifacts the store also has a jewelry outlet.

Antique lovers can also visit a number of other stores in the locality. The Piazza del Mercato – specializing in coins and stamps - is a popular antique market that is open on the third Sunday of every month. Located in Via

# SIENA TRAVEL GUIDE

Stalloreggi, the Bottega dell'Arte is the place to visit if one is looking for 14th and 15th century artwork copies.

## Bianco e Nero di Staccioli Sonia

Via dei Fusari 21

53100 Siena

Tel: +39 0577 28 00 26

http://www.biancoenero.it

Producing hand painted and completely lead-free ceramics, the Bianco e Niro is one of the best places to but ceramic handicrafts – one of the specialties of the region. Different shades of blue, green, and salmon are used to create artistic ceramics in a typical Sienese style. One can also order items online. It is owned and run by the Staciolli family that has been in the profession since the 15th century. The present store was opened in 1985.

# SIENA TRAVEL GUIDE

Ranging from plates and cups to coffee cup sets and cruets, this is the must-visit store for those who wish to take back some fine traditional handicrafts of Siena.

## Falegnameria Artistica

P. Nenni Loc Badesse

53035 Siena

Tel: +39 0577 30 43 00

http://www.falegnameria-artistica.it

This is a specialty store for wooden furniture and objects to be created in a perfect antique style and design. From small items like plate racks and bookstands to large products like beds and cabinets, the store has earned a name for its fine artwork and perfection in replicating designs from the past.

# SIENA TRAVEL GUIDE

The store often takes its products to the Pizza del Campo market for sale but one can find a larger variety in its store at Loc Badesse. A good place to swing by if one is looking to take back home something different.

## Via di Citta

Regarded as one of the most elegant streets in Siena, the Via di Citta – formerly known as Via Galgaria – displays Siena's history at its finest and is also known for its number of shops selling curios and local handicrafts. The street used to house many shoemakers. It rises up one of the city's three hills to a beautiful view of the town, including the Torre del Mangia.

On the street, one can find patrician estates such as the 14th century Palazzo Patrizzi and the 16th century Palazzo Marescotti, which now houses the Chigiana

# SIENA TRAVEL GUIDE

Musical Academy. It has the popular Ceramiche Artistiche Santa Caterina (No. 51) - a ceramic store known for its price-worthy product line – and a perfect place to buy souvenirs. The street also has high-end boutique stores like the Via Dei Montanini and Via Banchi di Sopra.

## Know Before You Go

# 🌐 Entry Requirements

By virtue of the Schengen agreement, travellers from other countries in the European Union do not need a visa when visiting Italy. Additionally Swiss travellers are also exempt. Visitors from certain other countries such as the USA, Canada, Japan, Israel, Australia and New Zealand do not need visas if their stay in Italy does not exceed 90 days. When entering Italy you will be required to make a declaration of presence, either at the airport, or at a police station within eight days of arrival. This applies to visitors from other Schengen countries, as well as those visiting from non-Schengen countries.

# 🌐 Health Insurance

Citizens of other EU countries are covered for emergency health care in Italy. UK residents, as well as visitors from Switzerland are covered by the European Health Insurance Card (EHIC), which can be applied for free of charge. Visitors from non-Schengen countries will need to show proof of private health insurance that is valid for the duration of their stay in

Italy (that offers at least €37,500 coverage), as part of their visa application. No special vaccinations are required.

# 🌐 Travelling with Pets

Italy participates in the Pet Travel Scheme (PETS) which allows UK residents to travel with their pets without requiring quarantine upon re-entry. Certain conditions will need to be met. The animal will have to be microchipped and up to date on rabies vaccinations. In the case of dogs, a vaccination against canine distemper is also required by the Italian authorities. When travelling from the USA, your pet will need to be microchipped or marked with an identifying tattoo and up to date on rabies vaccinations. An EU Annex IV Veterinary Certificate for Italy will need to be issued by an accredited veterinarian. On arrival in Italy, you can apply for an EU pet passport to ease your travel in other EU countries.

# 🌐 Airports

**Fiumicino – Leonardo da Vinci International Airport** (FCO) is one of the busiest airports in Europe and the main international airport of Italy. It is located about 35km southwest of the historical quarter of Rome. Terminal 5 is used for trans-Atlantic and international flights, while Terminals 1, 2 and 3 serve mainly for domestic flights and medium haul flights to

## SIENA TRAVEL GUIDE

other European destinations. Before Leonardo da Vinci replaced it, the **Ciampino–G. B. Pastine International Airport** (CIA) was the main international airport servicing Rome and Italy. It is one of the oldest airports in the country still in use. Although it declined in importance, budget airlines such as Ryanair boosted its air traffic in recent years. The airport is used by Wizz Air, V Bird, Helvetic, Transavia Airlines, Sterling, Ryanair, Thomsonfly, EasyJet, Air Berlin, Hapag-Lloyd Express and Carpatair.

**Milan Malpensa Airport** (MXP) is the largest of the three airports serving the city of Milan. Located about 40km northwest of Milan's city center, it connects travellers to the regions of Lombardy, Piedmont and Liguria. **Milan Linate Airport** (LIN) is Milan's second international airport. **Venice Marco Polo Airport** (VCE) provides access to the charms of Venice. **Olbia Costa Smeralda Airport** (OLB) is located near Olbia, Sardinia. Main regional airports are **Guglielmo Marconi Airport** (BLQ), an international airport servicing the region of Bologna, **Capodichino Airport** at Naples (NAP), **Pisa International Airport** (PSA), formerly Galileo Galilei Airport, the main airport serving Tuscany, **Sandro Pertini Airport** near Turin (TRN), **Cristoforo Colombo** in Genoa (GOA), **Punta Raisi Airport** in Palermo (PMO), **Vincenzo Bellini Airport** in Catania (CTA) and **Palese Airport** in Bari (BRI).

# SIENA TRAVEL GUIDE

## 🌐 Airlines

Alitalia is the flag carrier and national airline of Italy. It has a subsidiary, Alitalia CityLiner, which operates short-haul regional flights. Air Dolomiti is a regional Italian based subsidiary of of the Lufthansa Group. Meridiana is a privately owned airline based at Olbia in Sardinia.

Fiumicino - Leonardo da Vinci International Airport serves as the main hub for Alitalia, which has secondary hubs at Milan Linate and Milan Malpensa Airport. Alitalia CityLiner uses Fiumicino – Leonardo da Vinci International Airport as main hub and has secondary hubs at Milan-Linate, Naples and Trieste. Fiumicino – Leonardo da Vinci International Airport is also one of two primary hubs used by the budget Spanish airline Vueling. Milan Malpensa Airport is one of the largest bases for the British budget airline EasyJet. Venice Airport serves as an Italian base for the Spanish budget airline, Volotea, which provides connections mainly to other destinations in Europe. Olbia Costa Smeralda Airport (OLB), located near Olbia, Sardinia is the primary base of Meridiana, a private Italian Airline in partnership with Air Italia and Fly Egypt.

## 🌐 Currency

Italy's currency is the Euro. It is issued in notes in denominations of €500, €200, €100, €50, €20, €10 and €5.

Coins are issued in denominations of €2, €1, 50c, 20c, 10c, 5c, 2c and 1c.

## 🌐 Banking & ATMs

Using ATMs or Bancomats, as they are known in Italy, to withdraw money is simple if your ATM card is compatible with the MasterCard/Cirrus or Visa/Plus networks. There is a €250 limit on daily withdrawals. Italian machines are configured for 4-digit PIN numbers, although some machines will be able to handle longer PIN numbers. Bear in mind some Bancomats can run out of cash over weekends and that the more remote villages may not have adequate banking facilities so plan ahead.

## 🌐 Credit Cards

Credit cards are valid tender in most Italian businesses. While Visa and MasterCard are accepted universally, most tourist oriented businesses also accept American Express and Diners Club. Credit cards issued in Europe are smart cards that that are fitted with a microchip and require a PIN for each transaction. This means that a few ticket machines, self-service vendors and other businesses may not be configured to accept the older magnetic strip credit cards. Do remember to advise your bank or credit card company of your travel plans before leaving.

## 🌐 Tourist Taxes

Tourist tax varies from city to city, as each municipality sets its own rate. The money is collected by your accommodation and depends on the standard of accommodation. A five star establishment will levy a higher amount than a four star or three star establishment. You can expect to pay somewhere between €1 and €7 per night, with popular destinations like Rome, Venice, Milan and Florence charging a higher overall rate. In some regions, the rate is also adjusted seasonally. Children are usually exempt until at least the age of 10 and sometimes up to the age of 18. In certain areas, disabled persons and their companions also qualify for discounted rates. Tourist tax is payable directly to the hotel or guesthouse before the end of your stay.

## 🌐 Reclaiming VAT

If you are not from the European Union, you can claim back VAT (Value Added Tax) paid on your purchases in Italy. The VAT rate in Italy is 21 percent and this can be claimed back on your purchases if certain conditions are met. The merchant needs to be partnered with a VAT refund program. This will be indicated if the shop displays a "Tax Free" sign. The shop assistant will fill out a form for reclaiming VAT. When you submit this at the airport, you will receive your refund.

# 🌐 Tipping Policy

If your bill includes the phrase "coperto e servizio", that means that a service charge or tip is already included. Most waiting staff in Italy are salaried workers, but if the service is excellent, a few euros extra would be appreciated.

# 🌐 Mobile Phones

Most EU countries, including Italy use the GSM mobile service. This means that most UK phones and some US and Canadian phones and mobile devices will work in Italy. While you could check with your service provider about coverage before you leave, using your own service in roaming mode will involve additional costs. The alternative is to purchase an Italian SIM card to use during your stay in Italy.

Italy has four mobile networks. They are TIM, Wind, Vodafone and Tre (3) and they all provide pre-paid services. TIM offers two tourist options, both priced at €20 (+ €10 for the SIM card) with a choice of two packages - 2Gb data, plus 200 minutes call time or internet access only with a data allowance of 5Gb. Vodafone, Italy's second largest network offers a Vodafone Holiday package including SIM card for €30. They also offer the cheapest roaming rates. Wind offers an Italian Tourist pass for €20 which includes 100 minutes call time and 2Gb data and can be extended with a restart option for an extra €10.

To purchase a local SIM card, you will need to show your passport or some other form of identification and provide your residential details in Italy. By law, SIM registration is required prior to activation. Most Italian SIM cards expire after a 90 day period of inactivity. When dialling internationally, remember to use the (+) sign and the code of the country you are connecting to.

## 🌐 Dialling Code

The international dialling code for Italy is +39.

## 🌐 Emergency Numbers

Police: 113
Fire: 115
Ambulance: 118
MasterCard: 800 789 525
Visa: 800 819 014

## 🌐 Public Holidays

1 January: New Year's Day (Capodanno)
6 January: Day of the Epiphany (Epifania)
March-April: Easter Monday (Lunedì dell'Angelo or Pasquetta)
25 April: Liberation Day (Festa della Liberazione)

## SIENA TRAVEL GUIDE

1 May: International Worker's Day (Festa del Lavoro / Festa dei Lavoratori)

2 June: Republic Day (Festa della Repubblica)

15 August: Assumption Day (Ferragosto / Assunta)

1 November: All Saints Day (Tutti i santi / Ognissanti)

8 December: Immaculate Conception (Immacolata Concezione / Immacolata)

25 December: Christmas Day (Natale)

26 December: St Stephen's Day (Santo Stefano)

A number of Saints days are observed regionally throughout the year.

# Time Zone

Italy falls in the Central European Time Zone. This can be calculated as Greenwich Mean Time/Coordinated Universal Time (GMT/UTC) +2; Eastern Standard Time (North America) -6; Pacific Standard Time (North America) -9.

# Daylight Savings Time

Clocks are set forward one hour on 29 March and set back one hour on 25 October for Daylight Savings Time.

# SIENA TRAVEL GUIDE

# 🌐 School Holidays

The academic year begins in mid September and ends in mid June. The summer holiday is from mid June to mid September, although the exact times may vary according to region. There are short breaks around Christmas and New Year and also during Easter. Some regions such as Venice and Trentino have an additional break during February for the carnival season.

# 🌐 Trading Hours

Trading hours for the majority of shops are from 9am to 12.30pm and then again from 3.30pm to 7.30pm, although in some areas, the second shift may be from 4pm to 8pm instead. The period between 1pm and 4pm is known in Italy as the *riposo*. Large department shops and malls tend to be open from 9am to 9pm, from Monday to Saturday. Post offices are open from 8.30am to 1.30pm from Monday to Saturday. Most shops and many restaurants are closed on Sundays. Banking hours are from 8.30am to 1.30pm and then again from 3pm to 4pm, Monday to Friday. Most restaurants are open from noon till 2.30pm and then again from 7pm till 11pm or midnight, depending on the establishment. Nightclubs open around 10pm, but only liven up after midnight. Closing times vary, but will generally be between 2am and 4am. Museum hours vary, although major sights tend to be open continuously and often up to 7.30pm. Many museums are closed on Mondays.

## 🌐 Driving Laws

The Italians drive on the right hand side of the road. A driver's licence from any of the European Union member countries is valid in Italy. Visitors from non-EU countries will require an International Driving Permit that must remain current throughout the duration of their stay in Italy.

The speed limit on Italy's autostrade is 130km per hour and 110km per hour on main extra-urban roads, but this is reduced by 20km to 110km and 90km respectively in rainy weather. On secondary extra-urban roads, the speed limit is 90km per hour; on urban highways, it is 70km per hour and on urban roads, the speed limit is 50km per hour. You are not allowed to drive in the ZTL or Limited Traffic Zone (or *zona traffico limitato* in Italian) unless you have a special permit.

Visitors to Italy are allowed to drive their own non-Italian vehicles in the country for a period of up to six months. After this, they will be required to obtain Italian registration with Italian licence plates. Italy has very strict laws against driving under the influence of alcohol. The blood alcohol limit is 0.05 and drivers caught above the limit face penalties such as fines of up to €6000, confiscation of their vehicles, suspension of their licenses and imprisonment of up to 6 months. Breathalyzer tests are routine at accident scenes.

## 🌐 Drinking Laws

The legal drinking age in Italy is 16. While drinking in public spaces is allowed, public drunkenness is not tolerated. Alcohol is sold in bars, wine shops, liquor stores and grocery shops.

## 🌐 Smoking Laws

In 2005, Italy implemented a policy banning smoking from public places such as bars, restaurants, nightclubs and working places, limiting it to specially designated smoking rooms. Further legislation banning smoking from parks, beaches and stadiums is being explored.

## 🌐 Electricity

Electricity: 220 volts

Frequency: 50 Hz

Italian electricity sockets are compatible with the Type L plugs, a plug that features three round pins or prongs, arranged in a straight line. An alternate is the two-pronged Type C Euro adaptor. If travelling from the USA, you will need a power converter or transformer to convert the voltage from 220 to 110, to avoid damage to your appliances. The latest models of many laptops, camcorders, mobile phones and digital cameras are dual-voltage with a built in converter.

## 🌐 Tourist Information (TI)

There are tourist information (TI) desks at each of the terminals of the Leonardo da Vinci International Airport, as well as interactive Information kiosks with the latest touch-screen technology. In Rome, the tourist office can be found at 5 Via Parigi, near the Termini Station and it is identified as APT, which stands for Azienda provinciale del Turismo. Free maps and brochures of current events are available from tourist kiosks.

Several of the more tourist-oriented regions of Italy offer tourist cards that include admission to most of the city's attractions. While these cards are not free, some offer great value for money. A variety of tourism apps are also available online.

## 🌐 Food & Drink

Pasta is a central element of many typically Italian dishes, but there are regional varieties and different types of pasta are matched to different sauces. Well known pasta dishes such as lasagne and bolognaise originated in Bologna. Stuffed pasta is popular in the northern part of Italy, while the abundance of seafood and olives influences southern Italian cuisine. As far as pizza goes, the Italians differentiate between the thicker Neapolitan pizza and the thin crust Roman pizza, as well as white pizza, also known as focaccia and tomato based pizza. Other standards include minestrone soup, risotto, polenta and a variety of cheeses, hams, sausages and salamis. If you are on a budget, consider snacking on stuzzichini with a few drinks during happy hour which is often between 7 and 9pm. The fare can include salami, cheeses, cured meat, mini pizzas, bread, vegetables, pastries or pate. In Italy, Parmesan refers only to cheese originating from the area surrounding Parma. Favorites desserts include tiramisu or Italian gelato.

Italians enjoy relaxing to aperitifs before they settle down to a meal and their favorites are Campari, Aperol or Negroni, the famous Italian cocktail. Wine is enjoyed with dinner. Italy is particularly famous for its red wines. The best known wine regions are Piedmont, which produces robust and dry reds, Tuscany and Alto Adige, where Alpine soil adds a distinctive acidity. After the meal, they settle down to a glass of limoncello, the country's most popular liqueur, or grappa, which is distilled from grape seeds and stems, as digestive. Other options in this class include a nut liqueur, nocino, strawberry based Fragolino Veneto or herbal digestives like gineprino, laurino or mirto. Italians are also fond of coffee. Espresso is drunk through throughout the day, but cappuccino is considered

# SIENA TRAVEL GUIDE

a morning drink. The most popular beers in Italy are Peroni and Moretti.

## 🌐 Websites

http://vistoperitalia.esteri.it/home/en

This is the website of the Consulate General of Italy. Here you can look up whether you will need a visa and also process your application online.

http://www.italia.it/en/home.html

The official website of Italian tourism

http://www.italia.it/en/useful-info/mobile-apps.html

Select the region of your choice to download a useful mobile app to your phone.

http://www.italylogue.com/tourism

http://italiantourism.com/index.html

http://www.reidsitaly.com/

http://wikitravel.org/en/Italy

https://www.summerinitaly.com/

http://www.accessibleitalianholiday.com/

Planning Italian vacations around the needs of disabled tourists.

Printed in Great Britain
by Amazon